Original title:
Aurora Glow

Copyright © 2024 Swan Charm
All rights reserved.

Author: Kätriin Kaldaru
ISBN HARDBACK: 978-9916-79-558-3
ISBN PAPERBACK: 978-9916-79-559-0
ISBN EBOOK: 978-9916-79-560-6

The Glow of New Beginnings

In the hush of the dawn, a promise is born,
The world awakens, fresh and adorned.
Each breath a chance, each step a dream,
Life whispers softly, like a gentle stream.

With colors of hope, the sky starts to change,
Old worries fade, while futures rearrange.
Embrace the light, let shadows release,
A canvas awaits, where hearts find their peace.

Morning's Gentle Caress

The sun peeks shyly, kissing the earth,
Soft golden rays, celebrating rebirth.
Birds sing sweetly, in melodic delight,
Their tunes weave magic in the soft morning light.

Mist dances lightly over fields of green,
Each droplet sparkling, a glimmering sheen.
Time slows down in this warm, tender glow,
As day unfolds softly, with promises to sow.

Horizon's Whispering Flames

The horizon ignites with a fiery embrace,
Colors collide in a vibrant space.
Whispers of dreams ride the wafting breeze,
Stories unfold with such effortless ease.

Each flicker of light tells tales of the past,
A dance of the present, too wild to last.
Hope rises high, like embers in flight,
Illuminating paths in the cloak of night.

Shimmering Threads of Dawn

Threads of gold weave through the sky,
Each moment cherished, as hours drift by.
Nature awakens, a symphony plays,
In the woven fabric of brightening days.

A tapestry rich with stories untold,
In every hue of silver and gold.
Hearts dance to rhythms, serene and profound,
In the gentle embrace of mornings unbound.

Embrace of the Fading Night

As shadows stretch across the ground,
Whispers of silence begin to sound.
Stars peek through the velvet sky,
Night's embrace, a soft lullaby.

Moonlight dances on the trees,
Carrying secrets in the breeze.
Dreams awaken from their flight,
In the arms of the fading night.

Twilight's Last Breath

Hues of purple and gold collide,
As day gives in, with dreams to bide.
The sun descends, a gentle sigh,
Twilight's last breath, a sweet goodbye.

Birds retreat to nests of rest,
Nature whispers, knows what's best.
In the hush, the night unfolds,
Twilight, a tale of love retold.

Glimmers in the Gloom

Amidst the dark, soft glimmers spark,
A flicker bright, defying stark.
In the gloom, the heart will soar,
Hope ignites, forevermore.

Shadows linger, yet light remains,
In quiet spaces, love sustains.
Dancing shimmers, pure and bright,
Glimmers found in endless night.

The Dawn's Gentle Caress

With every ray, the dark recedes,
A tender touch, the heart it feeds.
   Morning whispers in the air,
The dawn's gentle caress, so rare.

Colors bloom, the world awakes,
Soft light bathes the gentle lakes.
   Promises dwell in every hue,
The dawn's embrace, forever new.

The Light That Ignites

In shadows deep, a spark appears,
Whispers of hope, allay our fears.
A flicker bold, it starts to glow,
The heart, once dark, begins to know.

With every pulse, it starts to rise,
A flame of joy beneath the skies.
It dances soft, it flickers bright,
Transforming darkness into light.

Dawn's Opal Dance

Gentle hues of pink and gold,
A story new, waiting to unfold.
The sky awakes with hues so rare,
A dance of colors fills the air.

With every ray, the shadows melt,
In morning's grace, our hearts are felt.
The world ignites with vibrant glow,
As sunlight paints the earth below.

Colors of a Dreaming World

In a realm where wishes blend,
Reality bends, the colors send.
A canvas wide, brushed with delight,
Dreams emerge, taking flight.

Whirling shades of blue and green,
Imagination reigns supreme.
Each stroke brings a tale to weave,
In this world, we dare believe.

Resplendent Sunlit Canvas

Upon the hills, the sun cascades,
A tapestry where light parades.
Each blade of grass, a story spun,
Beneath the glow of day begun.

With every hue, the day evolves,
Nature's palette, it resolves.
In harmony, the colors blend,
A masterpiece that has no end.

The Rise of Infinite Colors

Beneath the dawn, the canvas awakes,
Brushstrokes of warmth spill across the lakes.
Crimson and gold dance in the light,
Whispers of beauty, a marvelous sight.

Fields of wildflowers, vibrant and free,
Each bloom a story, a symphony.
Emerald leaves in the gentle breeze,
Nature's palette, a heart to please.

Storm clouds gather, transforming the sky,
Shades of depression, a sorrowful sigh.
Yet after the rain, a rainbow's embrace,
Promises linger, a hopeful trace.

Stars awaken in the velvet night,
Colors of dreams take their majestic flight.
The universe twinkles, ever so bright,
Infinite wonders, a timeless delight.

In every corner, hues intertwine,
The rise of colors, a world divine.
Embrace the spectrum, let it unfold,
A journey of magic, a story told.

A Glimpse Beyond the Veil

Shadows dance softly in the pale moonlight,
Whispers of secrets, hidden from sight.
A veil of silence, thickening air,
Promises linger, cloaked in despair.

Cracks in the darkness, light filters in,
Murmurs of hope where shadows have been.
A flicker of truth, just out of reach,
Lessons in silence, the heart will teach.

Through the misty haze, a figure appears,
Riddles of time mingled with fears.
Each layer peeled back reveals a new song,
A tapestry woven, where we all belong.

Glimpses of wisdom shine bright and bold,
Stories of ages, in silence, told.
Beyond the veil, magic lays still,
A promise of answers, a thirst to fulfill.

In twilight's embrace, shadows lay low,
A dance with the unknown, we learn to flow.
Trust the journey, let your spirit sail,
Discover the wonders, a glimpse beyond the veil.

Ethereal Dawn Revelations

In the hush of morning's grace,
Whispers dance on soft, cool air.
Veils of light begin to chase,
Night's shadow, fading everywhere.

Birds sing out in sweet delight,
Colors bloom, a vivid wake.
Nature stirs from restful night,
Promises of beauty, we partake.

Misty hues in gardens glow,
Petals glisten with the dew.
Laughter threads the breezy flow,
A world reborn, fresh and new.

Clouds drift softly, poised and high,
Carving paths in skies so blue.
Glistening orbs of sunlight fly,
Kissing earth in golden hue.

Celestial Rays Emerging

As dawn unfolds her tender light,
Celestial rays break through the gloom.
Every shadow takes to flight,
Chasing dreams from night's cold tomb.

Beneath the arch of azure skies,
Each ray whispers secrets untold.
Eyes awaken, hearts arise,
In the warmth, we feel consoled.

Silhouettes in brilliant hues,
Joyous cries in nature's choir.
Harmony in morning's muse,
Ignites within a bright desire.

Rippling streams reflect the sun,
Nature's canvas bursts with glee.
In each moment, life has spun,
A story waiting to be free.

Palette of the Breaking Day

Awake to nature's soft embrace,
Palette rich with colors bold.
Brushstrokes dance in gentle grace,
Whispers of a tale retold.

Amber rays and tangerine,
Flutter through the branches wide.
Cascading light, a sight serene,
Filling hearts with joy inside.

Scarlet blooms against the green,
Every petal tells a dream.
In the quiet moments seen,
Life's rich tapestry does gleam.

Morning dew on blades of grass,
Sparkles like a thousand stars.
As the fleeting moments pass,
Nature's wonders leave their marks.

Harmonies of Radiance

Softly sings the dawn today,
Harmonies in every beat.
Whispers of the night give way,
To a melody so sweet.

Birdsongs weave through emerald trees,
Notes of joy in every breeze.
Dancing leaves and buzzing bees,
Nature's music aims to please.

In the glow of breaking morn,
Fingers stretch to greet the light.
With each note, new hopes are born,
Turning darkness into bright.

Sunrise paints the world anew,
Blending shades of warmth and care.
In this symphony of hue,
Life awakens everywhere.

Spectrum of Awakening Dreams

In the dawn's embrace, colors swirl,
Whispers of hope in each unfurl.
A canvas alive with soft, muted hues,
Awakening dreams, a world to choose.

Sunlight dances on dewy grass,
Carrying secrets as moments pass.
The gentle breeze sings soft and low,
Awakening dreams, causing hearts to glow.

Clouds drift slowly, painting the sky,
Echoes of laughter, a joyful sigh.
Silhouettes of trees sway in delight,
Awakening dreams, from day to night.

Stars twinkle bright, guiding the way,
In this vast expanse where shadows play.
With each heartbeat, a story to weave,
Awakening dreams, the mind shall conceive.

As evening falls and colors fade,
A tapestry woven in the glade.
With open hearts, we look to the night,
Awakening dreams, our spirits take flight.

A Symphony in Color

In the garden, colors burst alive,
A symphony vibrant, where dreams thrive.
Petals unfold, a melodic grace,
Nature's own rhythm, an endless embrace.

Whispers of blue and hints of gold,
Tales of the sun, through time retold.
Every shade sings a note so sweet,
In this grand concert, our hearts repeat.

The rustling leaves in harmony sway,
Conducting the breeze in a playful display.
Crimson and emerald, a lush delight,
A symphony in color, through day and night.

As twilight descends, the notes take flight,
A canvas of stars ignites the night.
Each hue a memory, each sound a dream,
A symphony in color, flowing like a stream.

With every heartbeat, a masterpiece blooms,
In this lyrical garden, life resumes.
Together we dance, hearts set free,
In the symphony of color, just you and me.

Revelry in the Heavens

The stars align in joyful arrays,
A celestial dance in the Milky Way.
Cosmic whispers echo far and near,
In revelry, the heavens hold dear.

Galaxies twirl like ribbons of light,
Painting the darkness, a breathtaking sight.
Nebulas bloom, like flowers so rare,
In this cosmic fest, we are all aware.

Comets streak by in jubilant trails,
As stardust drifts on celestial gales.
Planets spin softly, in gentle embrace,
Revelry in the heavens, a timeless space.

Moonlight cascades on the earth below,
A silver party where shadows glow.
With every heartbeat, our spirits unite,
In revelry, we dance through the night.

As dawn approaches, the celebrations cease,
Yet the memories linger, bringing us peace.
In the quiet moments, we know our place,
Revelry in the heavens, a loving grace.

The Sky's Painted Secrets

As daylight wanes, the sky transforms,
Brushstrokes of pink and orange norms.
Secrets of the twilight come to play,
In the hues of dusk, they softly sway.

Clouds drift gently, a canvas adorned,
Tales of the sun, in colors, are formed.
Each sunset whispers a story untold,
The sky's painted secrets, in beauty bold.

Stars awaken, revealing their song,
In the tapestry of night, where we belong.
A symphony crafted by dreams and light,
The sky's painted secrets, shining so bright.

Every moment holds a glimmer of grace,
In the ever-changing, vast space.
With open hearts and gazes up high,
The sky's painted secrets fulfill our sigh.

As night unfolds, we wander and roam,
In the embrace of the universe, we find home.
Each glance at the heavens, a comforting guide,
The sky's painted secrets, with us abide.

Lullabies in the Light

Soft whispers hum in the night,
While the stars twinkle with delight.
Gentle breezes start to sway,
Carrying dreams till break of day.

Moonlit shadows dance and play,
Holding secrets, soft and gray.
Murmurs of a world so bright,
Sending lullabies in the light.

In tender moments, time will pause,
Nature sings without a cause.
Crickets chirp their soft refrain,
As sleep wraps round like gentle rain.

Through the veil of silent skies,
A symphony of sweet goodbyes.
The dawn will rise with colors bold,
But for now, the night is gold.

Close your eyes and drift away,
In the warmth of dreams, we'll stay.
Lullabies we hold so tight,
In the cradle of the night.

Chiaroscuro of Awakening

In shadows deep, the light breaks through,
A contrast sharp of old and new.
Silent whispers call the day,
As dreams begin to drift away.

Softly, the palette starts to blaze,
In hues that speak of gentle ways.
The morning stretches, soft and slow,
Illuminating all below.

With every hue, the world ignites,
Transforming dark to brilliant sights.
The dance of light upon the ground,
In chiaroscuro, life's profound.

Awake, awake! The call is clear,
Embrace the warmth, dispel the fear.
Let colors brighten every heart,
In dawn's embrace, we play our part.

This new canvas welcomes grace,
In every corner, we find our space.
Awakening brings forth the light,
In the chiaroscuro, day takes flight.

Dawn's First Embrace

The night surrenders, stars still fade,
As dawn unfolds its gentle braid.
Softest blush across the land,
Nature wakes to morning's hand.

Whispers linger in the air,
As sunlight kisses everywhere.
Birds begin to sing their song,
In harmony, the world belongs.

Golden rays greet every face,
Inviting joy in their embrace.
The dew-kissed grass, a precious sight,
Reflects the warmth of morning light.

Awakening to colors bright,
The earth unfolds from dark to light.
With every breath, a fresh start blooms,
As day dispels the evening's gloom.

In dawn's first hug, we breathe anew,
A canvas brushed with every hue.
Together we will greet the day,
In dawn's first embrace, we find our way.

The Light Before Time

In the realm where echoes rest,
Rays undulate, a subtle quest.
Timeless whispers form the air,
The light before, a silent prayer.

Waves of warmth through ages seep,
Binding moments, bright and deep.
In stillness, history unwinds,
Showing truths the heart still finds.

Before the clocks began to chime,
Dawn stood still, a space in time.
With every pulse, creation danced,
In light's embrace, we were entranced.

A place where shadows cease to roam,
In the light, we find our home.
Each glimmer sparkles with intent,
The light before is heaven-sent.

Breathe in deep and let it be,
This light before, a symphony.
In ageless glow, we hear the rhyme,
Of the light that draws us closer to time.

Secrets of the Shimmering Skies

Beneath the moon's soft glow, we tread,
Whispers of stars, secrets unsaid.
Twilight beckons, dreams take flight,
In the embrace of the velvet night.

Constellations weave tales so grand,
Ancient stories, hand in hand.
Each twinkle holds a hidden sign,
Guiding us through the divine.

The winds carry secrets from afar,
Echoes of light from a distant star.
As we gaze at the heavens so wide,
In their beauty, we confide.

A gentle breeze stirs the soul's deep core,
Hearts entwined, we long for more.
In the stillness of the night, we find,
The shimmering skies speak to the mind.

We dance among the light's embrace,
Finding solace in this sacred space.
Every secret held in a sigh,
Revealed at dawn, when shadows die.

Rhapsody in Rays

Morning breaks with golden hues,
Nature's symphony softly ensues.
Birds in chorus, joy takes flight,
Bathed in warmth, we greet the light.

Each ray that kisses the waking ground,
Brings forth magic all around.
Petals unfurl, colors ignite,
In this rhapsody of pure delight.

The world awakens, fresh and new,
Chasing shadows, embracing blue.
Harmonies play on the vibrant scene,
In the dance of nature, we glean.

With every step, we find our song,
In the rhythm of life, we belong.
Together we sway, hearts aligned,
Lost in the melody, love intertwined.

As daylight yields to twilight's glow,
The rhapsody whispers, soft and low.
In the echoes of day's sweet praise,
We linger in the warmth of rays.

A Dance Beyond Night

Silhouettes twirl in the dim-lit space,
Stars aligned, we find our grace.
Shadows flicker, dreams take form,
In the night's embrace, hearts are warm.

A beat resounds, the moon's bright stare,
We lose ourselves in the electric air.
Footsteps mingle, laughter rings,
In the depth of night, freedom sings.

With every twirl, we break the norm,
As constellations guide through the storm.
The dance of time, a fleeting chance,
Wrapped in wonder, we dare to dance.

Moments twine like vines that grow,
In this dance, we feel the flow.
When dawn approaches, we'll hold tight,
To the magic spun beyond the night.

For in this rhythm, we find our way,
Through shadows deep, where dreams will play.
A dance that speaks of love's delight,
Together we'll shine, through day and night.

Shattered Darkness

In the depths where shadows creep,
Silent whispers weave and seep.
Yet through the gloom, a spark ignites,
Shattered darkness, dancing lights.

Fractured echoes of hopes once lost,
Emerging flames, we bear the cost.
But from the ashes, courage grew,
In shattered darkness, strength breaks through.

Every tear shed, a glimmer found,
In the heart's chamber, solace abound.
Every heartbeat, a story told,
In the light's warmth, we become bold.

With every dawn, we rise anew,
Embracing colors, vibrant hue.
In unity, we find our voice,
Together we heal, together rejoice.

For darkness can never claim the day,
Love's light will always find a way.
Through shattered pieces, we will see,
The beauty of what's meant to be.

Glowing Horizons

In the dawn's first light, we rise,
Chasing dreams beneath the skies.
Colors blend, a vibrant sea,
Painting hope in harmony.

Whispers dance on gentle breeze,
The world awakens with such ease.
Golden rays, a soft caress,
Filling hearts with happiness.

Mountains stand, a silent guide,
Through valleys deep, where secrets hide.
Each step forward, a promise made,
In nature's arms, our fears allayed.

As horizons burst into flame,
We seek to know the world by name.
With every breath, we feel alive,
In glowing moments, we will thrive.

Hand in hand, we stroll the way,
Embracing what the skies convey.
Together, we'll make our stand,
On glowing horizons, hand in hand.

Enlightened Reverie

In dreams of light, we softly tread,
Where thoughts take flight and fear has fled.
Visions bloom in fields of gold,
Stories whispered, yet untold.

Moments gleam like morning dew,
Revealing shades of every hue.
With every heartbeat, spirits soar,
In enlightened realms, we seek for more.

A veil of peace drapes o'er the mind,
As stars align, their paths combined.
We follow trails of radiant grace,
Finding solace in this place.

The heart's desire sings in chorus,
In reveries that gently floor us.
From the depths, we rise anew,
With light's embrace, our journey true.

In twilight's glow, we pause and dream,
Life's beauty feels like sunlit stream.
Together we will find our way,
In enlightened reverie, we'll stay.

Dawn's Embrace

Awakening to gentle hues,
The world is fresh, soaked in the dews.
Morning whispers, tender and light,
Inviting souls to take their flight.

Golden beams stretch far and wide,
A promise of joy we cannot hide.
Each heartbeat dances in the air,
As dawn's embrace calls us to care.

Shapes of shadows softly bend,
In this stillness, find a friend.
Nature sings, a symphony,
In perfect tune, we feel so free.

The horizon blushes at our gaze,
As sunlight breaks the night's dark maze.
With open hearts, we greet the morn,
In dawn's embrace, our spirits born.

Through fields of hope, we gently roam,
In every step, we find our home.
With dawn's first light, we come alive,
In sacred grace, forever thrive.

Whispers of Celestial Light

Stars above in twinkling dance,
Invite our hearts to take a chance.
In midnight's hue, dreams intertwine,
Whispers of light, so pure, divine.

Moonbeams silver every stream,
Filling our minds with softest dream.
Galaxies spin in cosmic play,
Guiding our thoughts, lighting the way.

Gentle echoes of the night,
Calling us closer to the light.
In stillness, secrets start to shine,
Within the dark, our hopes align.

A tapestry of dreams unfolds,
In every thread, a story holds.
Embrace the whispers, let it be,
In celestial light, we set our spirits free.

Through the veil of night, we glide,
With every star, our hearts collide.
In the silence, we find our sight,
Embraced forever by the light.

The Lullaby of Dawn

Whispers of the night retreat,
As stars diminish, shadows meet.
The sky begins to blush and glow,
Awakening the world below.

Gentle breezes softly play,
A lullaby for break of day.
Nature stirs from evening's rest,
In dawn's embrace, we feel so blessed.

Colors blend in sweet refrain,
With every hue, joy breaks the chain.
Birds take flight on wings of song,
In this moment, we belong.

The silence fades, the light draws near,
In morning's breath, we shed all fear.
The symphony of day unfolds,
With stories new, and dreams retold.

So let the sun's warm embrace in,
Guide us forth, where hopes begin.
In dawn's soft light, we find our way,
Together we shall greet the day.

Splendor of the Morning Muse

A canvas brushed with golden light,
Inspiring hearts to take their flight.
With every ray, creativity flows,
In morning's warmth, the spirit grows.

The world adorned in vibrant hues,
Nature's palette, vast and true.
Flowers bloom with colors bright,
They dance beneath the morning light.

Mountains stand with grace and pride,
As rivers sing, and trees confide.
Each moment framed in beauty's gaze,
A hymn of life and heartfelt praise.

Awakened dreams begin to soar,
In the stillness, we explore.
The muse calls out, a siren's song,
In this new day, we all belong.

With whispers soft, the day unfolds,
In splendor bright, our story molds.
So let us rise and chase the muse,
In morning's glow, we cannot lose.

Flares of a New Day

Flares of light burst through the dark,
A spark ignites, awakening hearts.
The promise of a brand new start,
In every dawn, a joyous art.

The horizon glows with a golden hue,
As dreams emerge, vibrant and true.
Nature wakes with a gentle sigh,
While hopeful souls begin to fly.

Each breath a gift, each smile a sign,
In morning's arms, we intertwine.
Whispers of hope sing through the trees,
Carried away on the softest breeze.

Moments of stillness, tranquil delight,
As day unfolds, we find our light.
With each new ray, the magic stays,
In the flares of our bright new days.

So come forth, let your spirit soar,
Embrace the wonders, seek to explore.
For every dawn brings a chance to play,
In the flares of this beautiful day.

Cosmic Canvas Unfurled

A cosmic canvas stretched so wide,
Where galaxies and dreams collide.
Stars like brush strokes paint the night,
In silence deep, they share their light.

Nebulas in vibrant swirl,
With mysteries that softly unfurl.
The universe in endless dance,
Invites us all to take a chance.

Each twinkle tells a tale untold,
Of distant worlds and cosmic gold.
In starlit dreams, we drift away,
On constellations' gentle sway.

The moon whispers in silver tones,
As galaxies call us from our homes.
In this vast space, we find our place,
With every breath, we find our grace.

So let us gaze at the infinite sea,
Of dreams and wonders yet to be.
For in this cosmic embrace we dwell,
In the universe's timeless spell.

Chasing the First Rays

Morning breaks with gentle light,
A whisper soft, a sweet delight.
Birds begin their morning song,
As shadows fade, the day is strong.

Color spills across the sky,
Golden hues, they flutter high.
Awake the world from night's deep rest,
In dawn's embrace, we feel so blessed.

Through the trees, the sun peeks bright,
Painting dreams, igniting sight.
Each beam a promise, fresh and new,
Chasing rays, we seek the true.

The dew reflects the dawning glow,
Nature's canvas starts to flow.
With every step, we find our pace,
In morning's arms, we find our place.

As shadows dance and daylight dawns,
We chase the first rays on the lawns.
With hearts aligned to the sun's embrace,
We greet the world, our sacred space.

Luminescent Dreams

In the hush of nighttime's veil,
Whispers weave a timeless tale.
Stars above begin to gleam,
A tapestry of quiet dreams.

Silver beams like streams of light,
Illuminate the velvety night.
Each twinkle tells a secret wish,
Carried on the air we breathe.

Softly glows the moon's embrace,
Guiding wanderers through space.
With every sigh, a hope takes flight,
In luminescent dreams of night.

Each moment draped in glowing grace,
In shadows, find a sacred place.
We dance beneath the cosmic swirl,
In luminous dreams, our hearts unfurl.

Awake or lost in slumber's sway,
We find the magic in the gray.
With every heartbeat, dreams align,
In night's embrace, our spirits shine.

Palette of the Rising Sun

Brush the sky with shades so bold,
A canvas cast in blush and gold.
Splashes bright, a symphony,
A palette formed for all to see.

Rays of pink and orange blend,
Night's retreat, the dawn's sweet mend.
Nature holds the painter's brush,
In every hue, a vibrant rush.

Golden clusters burst with cheer,
In the silence, dreams draw near.
Every hue, a soft caress,
A morning song, our hearts express.

Soft clouds drift like whispered sighs,
As sunlight kisses waking eyes.
Colors dance as shadows flee,
In this art, we find our glee.

A masterpiece from night to day,
With each warm stroke, we find our way.
In this vivid world we play,
A palette bright, come what may.

Ethereal Dawn

Softly glows the morning light,
Awakening the world so bright.
Whispers float on gentle breeze,
In ethereal dawn, hearts find peace.

The mist unveils the verdant ground,
Where silence holds a sacred sound.
Each bloom unfolds, a promise made,
In dawn's embrace, all fears fade.

Colors bloom in radiant grace,
Nature's smile on every face.
With every heartbeat, life begins,
In ethereal dawn, our joy spins.

The sun ascends, a glowing orb,
Illuminating dreams to absorb.
With every light that breaks the night,
In dawn's embrace, we find our sight.

So let the morning's beauty prove,
In this ethereal dawn, we move.
Embracing each day with open arms,
In light we find our perfect charms.

Chasing Light Across the Sky

The sun breaks free from night's embrace,
Colors dance in morning's grace.
Shadows flee and dreams take flight,
We chase the warmth, we chase the light.

Clouds stretch high, like whispered sighs,
As laughter spills from open skies.
With every step, our spirits soar,
To greet the day and search for more.

Golden hues paint the landscape bright,
Every corner alive with light.
We run together, hearts in sync,
Finding joy in every blink.

Each moment fleeting, yet divine,
A promise held in the sunshine.
We chase our dreams, unfurling wide,
With hope and love, our faithful guide.

As twilight beckons, colors blend,
This dance of light, it's never end.
We chase the echoes of the day,
In every sunset, we find our way.

A Sunrise to Remember

Awake with dawn, the world feels new,
A canvas vast in shades of blue.
Soft whispers from the morning breeze,
A promise wrapped in sunlit trees.

Golden rays caress the earth,
A symphony of light and birth.
Birds sing sweet, their chorus bright,
In this moment, pure delight.

Shadows stretch as colors blend,
Morning's glow is a faithful friend.
Each heartbeat echoes, fresh and clear,
In the sunrise, we find our cheer.

With every sip of coffee brewed,
We gather dreams, our hearts renewed.
In this stillness, pause and see,
The beauty that sets our spirits free.

As sun climbs high, we hold it tight,
A sunrise cherished, pure and bright.
Let every dawn bring forth this grace,
In memories, we find our place.

The Color of Renewal

Life awakens after rain,
In the garden, joy remains.
Every petal, fresh and bright,
A promise held in nature's light.

Sprouts emerge with faces new,
Every shade in vibrant hue.
Hope unfurls in leafy form,
A dance of life, a lovely swarm.

Chasing shadows, finding days,
In the sunlight, love displays.
Colors blend, renew our sight,
In every blossom, sheer delight.

The earth rejoices in a song,
Where the gentle hearts belong.
Through the seasons, we shall know,
The color of renewal's glow.

With every breath, we find our place,
In the rhythm of nature's grace.
Life continues, strong and true,
In vibrant shades that carry you.

Glimmers from the Infinite Above

Stars scatter like dreams through night,
Glimmers whisper of ancient light.
In silence, the cosmos breathes,
A dance of hope upon the leaves.

The moon spills silver on the sea,
In her glow, we feel so free.
Each twinkle tells a story grand,
Of time and space, of where we stand.

A tapestry of dark and bright,
We search for meaning in the sight.
These glimmers guide us through the dark,
Each one a promise, each one a spark.

Wonders weave through the endless skies,
In their presence, our spirit flies.
We look above, our dreams take flight,
Chasing glimmers, embracing night.

In the stillness, hearts align,
With every star, a chance to shine.
Together, beneath this vast expanse,
We find connection in a cosmic dance.

Radiant Skies Awaken

The sun climbs high, so bold and bright,
Chasing away the cloak of night.
Colors burst in every hue,
The world awakens, fresh and new.

Birds take flight on gentle breeze,
Whispering through the rustling trees.
Nature sings its morning tune,
A symphony beneath the moon.

Flowers bloom with fragrant grace,
Painting joy in every space.
Radiant skies, a wondrous sight,
Heralding the day's delight.

Clouds drift lazily up above,
As sunlight pours like golden love.
With each ray, the shadows flee,
A promise of what's meant to be.

Embered Light Over the Horizon

The sun dips low, a fiery blaze,
Casting warmth through evening haze.
Embers flicker, soft and bright,
Whispering tales of day and night.

Mountains hold the fading light,
Guardians of the coming night.
Stars awaken, blinking slow,
As darkness weaves a velvet glow.

Echoes of the day recede,
Nature rests, its heart to heed.
Shadows stretch, they dance and play,
In the twilight, dreams hold sway.

Underneath the vast expanse,
Midnight stars in silent dance.
While embers fade to silent sighs,
New worlds spark in twinkling skies.

Northern Hues of Wonder

In the north, where silence reigns,
Beauty whispers through the plains.
Horizon paints in colors bright,
Nature's brush, a pure delight.

Lavender skies as day departs,
Filling all with gentle arts.
Reflections dance on icy streams,
As the land slips into dreams.

Pines standing tall, a noble crew,
Cradling whispers, ancient and true.
In every shadow, secrets hide,
A magical world where hopes abide.

As night unsettles, stars appear,
Twinkling diamonds, bright and clear.
In northern hues, we find our peace,
A breath of wonder, sweet release.

Ethereal Morning Canvas

A canvas fresh with morning's grace,
The dawn unfolds, a warm embrace.
Soft pastels brush the waking skies,
Painting dreams where daylight flies.

Mist dances lightly on the ground,
Whispers of dawn, a sacred sound.
Golden rays through leaves cascade,
In this moment, beauty's made.

Birds chatter sweetly, a choir's song,
In this realm, we all belong.
Each note a thread of light we weave,
In the fabric of what we believe.

Nature's kiss on velvet morn,
Life awakens, refreshed, reborn.
An ethereal masterpiece displayed,
In the heart of the day's parade.

A Tapestry of Dawn

The sun peeks through the veil of night,
Its golden threads weave soft and bright.
Whispers of warmth upon the air,
A new beginning everywhere.

Birds awaken in gentle song,
Nature hums, where hearts belong.
The world dressed in hues of gold,
Stories of life begin to unfold.

Fog dances lightly on the ground,
While dreams of night are gently drowned.
Each beam a promise, fresh and new,
A canvas painted in morning hue.

Celebrate the quiet grace,
As dawn unfolds in sweet embrace.
With every ray, a chance to grow,
In harmony, the flowers show.

Embrace the light that starts to play,
Chasing lingering shadows away.
In this tapestry of the morn,
New hopes and joys are reborn.

Enchanted Horizons

Where the sky meets the rolling sea,
Horizons stretch, wild and free.
Clouds dance with a silver gleam,
Painting paths for dreams to dream.

Waves whisper secrets of ancient lore,
As the sun dips low, a passionate score.
Each horizon holds a magic bright,
Binding day and silk-soft night.

Stars poke through the twilight air,
Stirring wonder, everywhere.
The moon's embrace a gentle call,
Inviting spirits to rise and fall.

Breezes carry the scent of lore,
While shadows dance on a sandy floor.
With every glance, a silent vow,
To cherish the beauty of the now.

In these enchanted lands we roam,
Finding peace, we make our home.
Horizons promise desires bright,
We follow softly into the night.

The Daybreak Sonata

A melody spills from the waking dawn,
Soft notes that linger, gently drawn.
With every ray that spills and sways,
The world awakens in harmonious ways.

Chirping birds join the symphony,
Crafting tunes of wild jubilee.
Leaves fluttering in the gentle breeze,
Nature's orchestra plays with ease.

The colors bloom like notes on a scale,
Transforming moments, telling a tale.
As sunbeams waltz through the morning mist,
Each heartbeat joins in the joyous list.

Every flower turns to the light,
In the warmth of this musical sight.
The daybreak sonata whispers sweet,
Lifting souls on dancing feet.

Join the rhythm, let spirits soar,
As dreams unfold from the ocean's core.
In every note, a promise lies,
The joy of life beneath the skies.

Murmurs of Tranquil Light

In quiet corners of morning's glow,
Murmurs of peace begin to show.
Soft rays filter through leafy trees,
Carrying whispers in the gentle breeze.

The world awakens with a tender sigh,
Underneath the vast, azure sky.
Where tranquility dances and takes its flight,
Cocooned in the warmth of tranquil light.

Ripples in streams reflect the calm,
Nature's beauty, an endless balm.
Gentle thoughts in the early hour,
Inviting hearts to bloom like flowers.

Each petal holds the stories untold,
Of life's journey, both brave and bold.
In this haven, we pause and see,
The gift of stillness, wild and free.

Let these murmurs fill the air,
Weaving dreams with tender care.
In tranquil light, our spirits sing,
Embracing all that morning brings.

Solstice Serenade

Whispers of the sun rise up,
As shadows dance and colors blush,
The longest day, a golden cup,
Filled with warmth, in nature's hush.

Through fields aglow with flowers bright,
The breeze hums soft, a gentle tune,
Embracing day, releasing night,
Underneath the watchful moon.

Laughter echoes, children play,
Underneath the skies so clear,
As twilight weaves into the gray,
The stars emerge, the night draws near.

Moments linger, time moves slow,
The light a brush on fading dreams,
Reveling in the sun's warm glow,
Life flows by in golden streams.

In every heart, the warmth remains,
A symphony of joy to find,
Through sunlit paths and gentle rains,
The solstice serenades the mind.

Echoes of Morning's Kiss

The dew drops glisten on the grass,
As dawn awakens with a sigh,
A tender moment, swift yet vast,
The world renewed beneath the sky.

Birds begin their morning song,
A melody that stirs the day,
As light spills forth and whispers strong,
Embracing all in warm array.

Sunbeams dance on trees so tall,
Casting shadows down the lane,
A quiet beauty, nature's call,
In every drop, love's sweet refrain.

Golden rays through window panes,
Awakening the dreams once spun,
In every heart, joy remains,
Echoes of a day begun.

With every breath, a promise new,
Of moments waiting to unfold,
In morning's kiss, a vibrant hue,
Life's cherished tales, forever told.

The Color of Awakening

Peachy hues light up the morn,
As night retreats with fading stars,
A canvas fresh, a world reborn,
The dawn extends its gentle arms.

In every petal, colors blend,
A palette bright upon the scene,
Nature's brush, a loyal friend,
Painting dreams where hearts have been.

Emerald leaves sway in the breeze,
With whispers of a new delight,
Awakening to memories,
Of tender hopes and blooming light.

Soft pastels of a waking day,
Embrace the earth with tender grace,
Each moment's hue, a sweet display,
Of life's embrace, a warm embrace.

Hope unfurls as morning breaks,
In every color, beauty found,
The world alights as nature wakes,
A vibrant symphony, profound.

Light's Tender Awakening

In the silence, dawn bestows,
A gentle touch, a lifting veil,
As light creeps in and softly glows,
Through shadows where dreams once sailed.

Golden rays that kiss the earth,
Awakening blossoms bold and bright,
In every moment, there's rebirth,
A celebration of morning light.

The sky, a canvas painted wide,
With strokes of pink and hues of blue,
A tranquil heart where peace can glide,
In every breath, the day feels new.

Fingers of warmth caress the trees,
As whispers dance on cool, fresh air,
The world unravels, and with ease,
New dreams awaken, free from care.

In light's embrace, we find our way,
With every dawn, a chance to rise,
To bask within the sun's warm play,
And greet the day with hopeful skies.

Soft Embrace of the Waking Sky

The dawn unfolds with tender grace,
Gentle whispers fill the space.
Birds awaken, songs take flight,
In soft embrace of morning light.

The clouds blush pink, a soft display,
As night retreats, it fades away.
The world stirs from a dream so deep,
In this moment, secrets keep.

Breezes carry scents anew,
Freshened earth, and vibrant hue.
The sun peeks in with golden rays,
Guiding hearts through morning's maze.

Each moment glows, a spark divine,
Nature dances, all align.
With open arms, the sky invites,
A journey starts in morning lights.

Soft shadows fade, the day ignites,
In radiant warmth, our spirit writes.
Embrace the light, let fears take flight,
In soft embrace of morning bright.

Hues of Celestial Time

Brush of colors paints the dawn,
A canvas wide, all fears are gone.
Crimson, gold, and azure rich,
Nature's art, a perfect stitch.

The sun ascends, a golden crown,
Over hillsides, through the town.
Each sunrise whispers tales untold,
In hues of warmth, both bright and bold.

Gentle breezes carry dreams,
In flowing streams and sunlight beams.
Time reveals its sacred toll,
Wielding brushstrokes on the soul.

As velvet night begins to fade,
Daybreak's promise, truth conveyed.
Nature's palette, boundless grace,
In each hue, we find our place.

The sky transforms, a wondrous scheme,
Chasing shadows, waking dreams.
In hues of celestial time we soar,
A dance of light forevermore.

Ritual of the Rising Light

In silence whispers dawn's soft call,
A ritual that enchants us all.
The horizon blushes, day begins,
Awakening dreams, where hope now spins.

The candles of stars extinguish slow,
As golden rays of warmth bestow.
In sync with nature, hearts align,
Through rituals of the rising shine.

With open arms, we greet the day,
The night recedes, it cannot stay.
Each moment glows, a sweet delight,
In the sacred dance of morning's light.

The earth awakens, life takes breath,
In every color, life conquers death.
A promise woven in the sky,
In the ritual of light, we rise high.

As shadows fade and spirits lift,
We celebrate this precious gift.
In harmony, the day ignites,
Within the ritual of endless lights.

New Day's Celestial Canvas

A new day dawns on canvas wide,
Brushstrokes of light in colors glide.
Purples bleed to vibrant gold,
Each sunrise new, a tale unfolds.

Layers of clouds, like dreams at play,
Concealing night, birthing day.
With every hue, a heartbeat sings,
In each soft whisper, possibility springs.

The sun awakes, a bright embrace,
Illuminating life in space.
Nature smiles as shadows part,
In the canvas of a hopeful heart.

As moments merge and time extends,
Our spirits rise, our journey bends.
In twilight's kiss, it finds its way,
On new day's canvas, bold display.

The world prepares for love's embrace,
In every corner, every place.
A masterpiece forever flows,
In new day's canvas, beauty grows.

The Light That Paints the World

In dawn's embrace, colors unfold,
Gentle whispers, stories told.
Brushstrokes soft on canvas bare,
Nature wakes with vibrant flair.

Shadows fade, the sun ascends,
Golden rays, the heart, it mends.
Fields of green and skies so blue,
Every hue feels fresh and new.

Mountains glow in morning light,
Cascading streams reflect the sight.
Petals bloom with rosy grace,
Life awakens, finds its place.

The world ignites, a vivid show,
In every corner, life will grow.
With each brush, the day begins,
In painted light, the joy within.

As twilight calls, the hues will blend,
A masterpiece that has no end.
The light that paints, forever stays,
In hearts and minds, throughout our days.

Fireworks of the Morning Sky

In morning's grip, the colors burst,
Petals sway, in dew they thirst.
A canvas bright with vibrant strife,
Nature's dance, a joyful life.

Crimson clouds in warm embrace,
Gold and orange interlace.
Each hue a spark of waking dreams,
Awakening the morning beams.

Birds take flight through azure space,
Chasing light at a lively pace.
Explosions of color fill the air,
As sunlight weaves without a care.

With every rise, a promise new,
In every heart, the visions brew.
Grounded in hope, our spirits soar,
Fireworks of light forevermore.

The morning sky, a vibrant play,
As daybreak breaks the edge of gray.
In this dance, our souls ignite,
A tapestry of pure delight.

Beneath the Veil of Light

Softly glows the evening's hue,
Underneath the sky so blue.
A gentle shroud of twilight's grace,
Each star, a dream, finds its place.

Whispers echo, shadows blend,
Time slows down, and hearts ascend.
Beneath this veil of silken light,
The world transforms, a sweet delight.

Moonlit paths where secrets dwell,
Nature spins her nightly spell.
In quietude, our thoughts take flight,
As we wander the realm of night.

Stars alight on velvet skies,
A symphony of silent sighs.
In every blink, a wish takes wing,
Beneath the light, our hopes will sing.

This sacred space, a healing sight,
Holding dreams in the soft twilight.
In the hush where spirits collide,
Beneath the veil, our hearts confide.

Flicker of Daybreak

A flicker stirs the quiet morn,
Rays of hope, a day reborn.
In whispers soft, the shadows sigh,
As colors bloom and dreams will fly.

Through the trees, light dances low,
Gentle waves in golden glow.
Each breath a gift, a sigh of peace,
In dawn's embrace, all worries cease.

The sky ignites with blush and flame,
Every dawn, a new acclaim.
With every flicker, hope ignites,
A symphony of morning lights.

In the stillness, hearts take flight,
Chasing dreams in morning's light.
With each dawn, the world will bloom,
Chasing shadows from the gloom.

Flicker bright, your promise calls,
Through the darkness, a love enthralls.
In daybreak's glow, we find our way,
With every dawn, a brand new day.

Awakening the Golden Hour

The sun dips slow, a glowing crown,
Painting the sky with shades of brown.
Birds take flight, their calls so clear,
In this moment, the world feels near.

Soft whispers brush the waking ground,
A golden warmth in every sound.
Trees stretch high with arms of grace,
Embracing light in this sacred space.

Clouds dissolve in hues divine,
This magic hour, where dreams align.
Time stands still, yet moves with ease,
Nature's breath is a gentle breeze.

Shadows lengthen, dance and swirl,
As day transforms in a gilded whirl.
Each heartbeat gains a brighter hue,
In this the golden hour, we renew.

With every glance, a story told,
In colors vivid, rich and bold.
Awakening souls from slumber's hold,
A promise whispered, softly unfold.

Spectral Embrace

Colors collide in vibrant streams,
A dance of light with endless dreams.
Each hue a whisper from above,
Nature's palette sings of love.

In the twilight, shadows blend,
Cascading light, a serene trend.
With every step, the spirits soar,
Touching the core, forevermore.

Mirrors glow with ghostly pride,
Reflections hide where secrets bide.
An embrace of shades in the night,
Guiding lost souls towards the light.

As stars awaken, softly gleam,
The cosmos hums a timeless theme.
In spectral realms, we lose our fears,
Wrapped in colors, soft as tears.

In this embrace, we find our place,
Bound by light in a gentle grace.
Every moment, a fleeting chance,
To join the dance, the spectral dance.

A Symphony of Light

A note is struck, the dawn ignites,
With colors dancing, pure delights.
The sun's embrace, a sweet refrain,
In every drop, the light retains.

Each ray a chorus, soft and bright,
Awakens dreams, dispels the night.
Nature's symphony, vast and clear,
Calls forth beauty, loud and near.

The whispers flow through trees so tall,
In harmony, they rise and fall.
Petals shimmer in morning's sigh,
A song of life, it fills the sky.

Across the field, shadows retreat,
As daylight steals the night's defeat.
In every heartbeat, rhythms weave,
A tapestry of light to believe.

A symphony shared, with time to spare,
In echoes vast, we find our prayer.
Together, we sing this celestial flight,
In wonder caught—our anthem bright.

Fading Shadows

As night descends, the colors pale,
Lingering whispers in the veil.
Shadows stretching, soft and long,
In this twilight, echoes belong.

Moonlight glimmers on silent lakes,
Every ripple, the night awakens.
Stars peep through with distant sight,
Guiding the lost to morning light.

In quiet corners, darkness weaves,
A gentle shroud, as daylight leaves.
Yet in this hush, a promise stays,
To greet the dawn in brighter ways.

A fleeting glance, the shadows play,
Leaving trails where dreams drift away.
In every heart, a flicker glows,
A reminder of what absence knows.

Tomorrow waits just out of frame,
To rekindle warmth, to fan the flame.
In fading night, we find our peace,
And from the dark, our hopes increase.

Rising Hues

The horizon blushes, bright and bold,
New beginnings in colors told.
With every breath, the dawn reveals,
A world awash in vibrant seals.

The canvas stretches far and wide,
As nature paints with heaven's pride.
Brushstrokes linger through the air,
With every sparkle, a whispered prayer.

Birds awaken, fill the skies,
In symphonies of joyful cries.
Each note a promise, loud and clear,
As life ascends, casting off fear.

The golden ray finds every tree,
In its embrace, where all is free.
Colors merge in a vivid hue,
A masterpiece of morning dew.

Rising hues, a spirit unleashed,\nIn this moment, all hearts are feasts.
Together we dance in the light's embrace,
In rising hues, we find our place.

Chasing the First Light

In the stillness of dawn's embrace,
Shadows flee as colors lace.
Whispers of hope in the air,
New beginnings, dreams laid bare.

The horizon blushes with gold,
Stories of wonders yet untold.
Sunrise blooms, a vivid swirl,
Awakening the sleepy world.

Birds take flight in joyous song,
Nature dances, wild and strong.
Every heartbeat whispers, 'Stay,'
Chasing light as night fades away.

Clouds drift softly in warm embrace,
Reflecting light, a gentle grace.
Morning dew on blades of grass,
Time slows down, a moment to pass.

So we chase the first light bright,
With open hearts, embracing sight.
Together we find our way,
Into the warmth of a new day.

Dance of the Cosmic Veil

Stars twinkle in a silent trance,
Galaxies whirl in a cosmic dance.
Nebulas swirl in colors bright,
Painting the canvas of the night.

Whispers of worlds far away,
Mysteries hide in night's ballet.
Every moment, a spell is cast,
Echoes of ages long since passed.

Two souls drift in the starlit sea,
Bound by fate, eternally free.
In the silence, secrets unfold,
The universe's heart is bold.

Comets blaze with fiery tails,
Charting paths through celestial trails.
Cosmic tides in a rhythmic swell,
Weaving a story only stars can tell.

As constellations start to gleam,
We lose ourselves in the dream.
Dancing under the cosmic veil,
In the universe, we shall prevail.

Awakening the Daydream

In the hush of morning's sigh,
Dreams emerge with a gentle cry.
Soft light spills on edges clear,
Awakening whispers, sweet and near.

Thoughts like petals drift and sway,
In a world where wishes play.
Imagination takes its flight,
Painting truths in colors bright.

Time stands still, a tender grace,
Each heartbeat finds its own place.
Cascading thoughts like a brook,
In every corner, life's new look.

Daydreams dance in golden rays,
Filling hearts with hopeful praise.
With every breath, worlds collide,
In the stillness, dreams abide.

We awaken to life's sweet call,
Embracing wonder, giving our all.
In daydreams, we find our way,
Guided by light of a brand-new day.

Twilight's Kiss Before Sunrise

In twilight's glow, the world holds still,
A hush descends, a tranquil will.
Stars blink softly, shadows creep,
Nature sighs, preparing for sleep.

The horizon blushes, colors blend,
A gentle promise, day will mend.
Moments suspended in the air,
Kissing the night with a tender care.

Night's embrace, a velvet sigh,
Whispers of dreams as they float by.
Crickets serenade, a lullaby,
Underneath the vast, starlit sky.

Each heartbeat echoes, breaths align,
Lost in the magic, divine design.
Twilight's kiss, a fleeting chance,
To savor peace in nature's dance.

As dawn approaches, lights will blend,
A cycle turns, the day ascends.
In twilight's arms, we find our peace,
A moment cherished, never cease.

Awakening with Every Color

In the dawn's tender embrace,
Colors bloom, a sweet trace.
Nature paints with graceful hand,
Awakening all across the land.

Violet whispers greet the sun,
In every shade, a race begun.
Golden rays stretch wide and far,
Guiding dreams, like a distant star.

Emerald leaves dance in the breeze,
Awakening hearts, putting minds at ease.
Every hue sings its own tune,
Under the watch of a gentle moon.

Crimson sighs of evening's glow,
Remind us of the day's sweet flow.
With each color, a story's told,
In every moment, love unfolds.

A canvas vast, life intertwines,
In shades of joy, the heart defines.
Awakening whispers in every hue,
A symphony of life, vibrant and true.

The Light of Endless Horizons

Beyond the hills, the sun will rise,
A dance of light across the skies.
Whispers of dawn, a soft caress,
Bringing with it hope, no less.

Waves of gold and amber glow,
Each morning gift, a fresh tableau.
In every sunrise, dreams take flight,
Setting the world alight.

Fingers of light stretch wide and free,
Touching hearts, a symphony.
Infinite views in tranquil grace,
Each horizon, a warm embrace.

As shadows fade, new paths unfold,
In the light, stories are told.
Every moment, a chance to see,
The beauty of life's endless decree.

Bathed in warmth, we stand as one,
Underneath a radiant sun.
Horizons vast, in splendid sight,
Together, we chase the light.

Song of the Morning Star

In the hush before the dawn,
A melody, sweetly drawn.
The morning star, a beacon bright,
Sings the world awake with light.

Notes of hope in the stillness flow,
Guiding dreams where spirits go.
With every twinkle, soft and clear,
A song of dawn that we all hear.

The sky blushes in gentle hues,
As night retreats, it softly views.
Together with the lark's first call,
We rise, we soar, we will not fall.

In every breath, the star's refrain,
A promise of joy, after pain.
Through gentle whispers, it imparts,
The strength to mend our weary hearts.

With the light of a brand new day,
We dance beneath its radiant sway.
In unity, we sing anew,
The song of life, forever true.

Faint Echoes of Morning's Light

In the quiet of daybreak's glow,
Faint echoes of night bid adieu.
Softly they whisper, tales untold,
In the warmth, shadows unfold.

The world awakens with tender grace,
As light begins its warm embrace.
Every corner filled with cheer,
Faint echoes beckoning us near.

Glistening dew, a jeweled crown,
Nature's laughter, a gentle sound.
With every breath, renewal sings,
As morning's light begins its wings.

Colors splash on canvas skies,
As old dreams fade, new ones rise.
In the rhythm of a heartbeat strong,
Faint echoes hum a brand new song.

With open arms, we greet the day,
In its arms, we long to stay.
Faint echoes now in harmony,
In morning's light, we are free.

The Spectrum of Silence

In shadows deep, whispers dwell,
A quiet truth, no words to tell.
Between the breaths, a soft refrain,
The hush of night, the echo of pain.

Colors fade in muted grace,
Silence weaves a tender lace.
Each secret sigh, a gentle breath,
In the calm, we dance with death.

Stars above in velvet skies,
Glimmers fade, the world complies.
In the dark, hearts softly sing,
In silence, life is whispered spring.

A gentle touch, a fleeting glance,
In quiet moments, souls may dance.
The spectrum speaks in shades of night,
Through silent shadows, find the light.

A fragile bond, unspoken ties,
In silence vast, our spirit flies.
The universe in stillness glows,
In whispered hues, the silence flows.

Hues of Hope

A painted sky, a dawn's embrace,
Soft pastels fill the wide space.
In every stroke, a dream unfurled,
With every color, a brand new world.

Emerald greens and golden rays,
In nature's palette, hope displays.
Each hue a promise, bright and clear,
In every heartbeat, love draws near.

A canvas fresh, a story told,
With vibrant tones, both brave and bold.
As shadows fade, new visions arise,
In hues of hope, the spirit flies.

The sun ascends, the morning sings,
Awakening the joy that brings.
Life blooms anew in every shade,
In nature's arms, our fears allayed.

Through every storm, through darkest night,
Hope glimmers like a distant light.
We forge ahead, our dreams in sight,
In hues of hope, we find our flight.

Dance of the Morning Light

The sun peeks through the curtain's seam,
A gentle glow, like a waking dream.
With tender rays, it paints the dawn,
In every hue, the night withdrawn.

The world awakens, soft and bright,
In the warm embrace of morning light.
Each blade of grass, a glistening gem,
Nature's beauty, a sacred hymn.

Birds take flight in joyful play,
Their melodies greet the new day.
In this dance, the heart takes wing,
In morning light, our souls will sing.

The sky ignites in orange and gold,
Stories of hope and love unfold.
With every breath, we feel alive,
In every moment, we will thrive.

The dance persists, as shadows fade,
In sunlight's warmth, fears are laid.
A celebration of life's delight,
In the dance of the morning light.

The Break of Day's Promise

With every dawn, a vow renewed,
The break of day in shades subdued.
Soft whispers in the waking breeze,
A gentle reminder of life's ease.

The horizon blushes, hope takes flight,
A tapestry woven with purest light.
As shadows linger, dreams collide,
In the promise of day, our souls abide.

Golden rays touch the earth's embrace,
In every corner, love finds its place.
With open hearts, we greet the morn,
In the break of day, new paths are born.

Every step beneath the sun,
The journey starts, the race begun.
With each new hour, we rise and sway,
In the break of day's promise, we find our way.

Together we'll chase the colors bright,
With every heartbeat, love ignites.
In the canvas of a brand new day,
The promise of life leads us to stay.

Veils of Celestial Radiance

In twilight's grasp, the stars ignite,
Softly draping the world in light.
Glimmers dance on the silent sea,
Veils of dreams, wild and free.

Whispers float in the fragrant air,
Each moment sings of secret care.
A tapestry spun from silver threads,
Guides our hearts where the starlight spreads.

Through gentle mists, the night unfolds,
Mysteries wrapped in shadows bold.
Celestial wonders, vast and near,
Paint the night with cosmic cheer.

As dawn approaches in soft embrace,
The veils dissolve with morning's grace.
Colors burst, a fiery blaze,
Veils of radiance, bright displays.

Underneath this celestial dome,
Hearts awaken, life finds home.
With each dawn, a canvas cast,
Veils of hope that hold us fast.

Mysteries of the Breaking Day

As twilight bows to morning's charm,
Secrets stir with a gentle calm.
A whisper runs through the waking trees,
Breath of dawn on a sultry breeze.

Nebulae hang like dreams in the air,
Nature's canvas, rich and rare.
Each ray of light, a brushstroke true,
Painting hills in a vibrant hue.

The owls retreat with soft goodbyes,
While hope awakens in sleepy eyes.
Shadows flee from the sun's warm plea,
World reborn in the light we see.

Fragments of night drip away slow,
Time unfurls with each gentle glow.
Mysteries dance as the birds take flight,
Heralds of joy in the morning light.

In dawn's embrace, dreams intertwine,
Life's rebirth, a sacred design.
The day unfolds, adventure to seek,
Hidden tales in the colors we speak.

Illuminated Whispers

In the gardens where shadows meet,
Softly echoing, secrets sweet.
Each petal glimmers, touched by gold,
Whispers of love, tender and bold.

Beneath the branches, light weaves a spell,
Stories murmured that time will tell.
Silent laughter dances on air,
Illuminated moments we share.

The brook babbles in sunlight's embrace,
Rippling tales of a hidden place.
Gentle breezes carry the sound,
Whispers of magic all around.

Embers of dusk begin to glow,
An ethereal pulse, a sacred flow.
Illuminated paths that twist and bend,
Guiding lost hearts, a faithful friend.

With every breath, the world confides,
Mysteries wrapped in nature's tides.
In every shadow, a glint remains,
Illuminated whispers in our veins.

Fragments of a New Day

When first light spills on the dewy land,
A canvas bright, painted by hand.
Fragments quilted from night's embrace,
Each thread woven, a gentle trace.

The world stirs softly, awake from dreams,
A chorus of birds and the sun's bright beams.
In the cool of morn, possibilities rise,
Fragments of hope fill the endless skies.

Glimmers of gold on the horizon's edge,
Promises whispered from nature's hedge.
Each moment glows with a fresh display,
Creating magic in the dawn's ballet.

Steps on the path of a brand new start,
Gathering courage with an open heart.
Fragments of laughter weave through the air,
Painting the day with love and care.

As shadows shrink and the sun ascends,
Life awakens, where time transcends.
With every heartbeat, a journey to lay,
In the fragments found within the day.

Echoes of the Rising Star

In the hush where shadows play,
Whispers of dawn drift away.
A star awakens, bright and near,
Its melody, a song we hear.

Through the night, it lights our path,
Illuminating dreams and math.
Each twinkle tells a tale untold,
Of mysteries in starlight bold.

Above the trees, it gently glows,
Warming hearts where silence flows.
A beacon of hope, fierce and bright,
Guiding souls through endless night.

Chasing echoes in the sky,
Daring hearts to dream and fly.
The rising star, our endless muse,
Calls us forth, we cannot lose.

In the stillness, we abide,
With every spark, our fears subside.
Together in the cosmic sea,
We find the light sets our spirit free.

Morning's Golden Wisp

A gentle breeze, the dawn unfurls,
As morning paints the world in pearls.
Golden rays through the window creep,
Awakening the day from sleep.

Birds are singing, notes in flight,
Chasing shadows from the night.
Softly wrapped in sunlit beams,
The heart awakens, lives its dreams.

In that glow, the flowers dance,
Each petal sways as if in trance.
Nature's chorus starts to swell,
In the magic, all is well.

Moments fleeting, yet so vast,
Yesterday melds with the past.
Time ticks gently, a wisp of grace,
In the morning's warm embrace.

As sun ascends, we greet the day,
With open arms, we find our way.
In every glow, the promise lies,
Of endless dreams beneath the skies.

Flashes of Sacred Splendor

In twilight's hold, a shimmer glows,
A sacred light, a tale it shows.
Each spark ignites the night's design,
Whispers of love, pure and divine.

Mighty mountains catch the gleam,
Reflecting hope in every beam.
In valleys deep where shadows creep,
The sacred flashes wake from sleep.

Leaves dance softly in the breeze,
Touched by light among the trees.
Every flicker tells a truth,
Ancient wisdom, ageless youth.

Moments captured, brief yet bright,
Scattered stars in the quiet night.
In the stillness, hearts expand,
Together, we will take a stand.

Through sacred spaces, spirits soar,
Embracing flashes, evermore.
In every heartbeat, every sight,
We find our way in sacred light.

The Infinite Light Horizon

Beyond where earth and sky collide,
An endless vision, free and wide.
Horizons stretch with every breath,
A journey starts with life and death.

In twilight's glow, the colors blend,
As day gives way to night's soft end.
A canvas vast, a space to dream,
Where every heart can share its gleam.

Each star a hope, a guiding sign,
Connected threads in a grand design.
The horizon beckons, calling clear,
An infinite journey, free from fear.

With every step, new paths unfold,
Stories waiting to be told.
In the stillness, we unite,
Boundless souls in the cosmic night.

Chasing shadows, light will guide,
Through the vast unknown, we won't hide.
For in the infinite, we find our song,
Together, we've always belonged.

Celestial Brushstrokes

Stars flicker in the deep,
Whispers of the night they keep.
Galaxies swirl in silent grace,
Painting light in endless space.

Comets trace a fleeting line,
Wonders wrapped in dark design.
Nebulas bloom like flowers bright,
In the cosmic canvas' flight.

The moon glows soft, a silver hue,
Casting shadows on the dew.
Constellations weave their tales,
Navigating celestial trails.

Each twinkle speaks of stories old,
Of brave hearts and dreams bold.
In the tapestry of night,
We find our place, our guiding light.

So gaze up high, let your heart soar,
In the universe, there's always more.
With every breath, let your spirit dance,
In the wonder of the cosmic expanse.

Luminous Dawn Serenade

Awakening with the golden hue,
Morning whispers, soft and new.
Birds lift songs, the world they greet,
In harmony, life's pulse, a beat.

Sunbeams stretch, they chase the night,
Painting hills in warming light.
Dewdrops sparkle like scattered gems,
Nature sings, the joy it stems.

Colors blend in vibrant plays,
A canvas born of night and days.
Clouds brush low, a gentle sigh,
As sunlight spreads across the sky.

Every shadow bids farewell,
In dawn's embrace, we find our spell.
With each heartbeat, hope takes flight,
In the promise of morning light.

Let your spirit rise and soar,
In this dance, forevermore.
Breathe in deeply the fresh morn,
In luminous whispers, we are reborn.

Fading Night's Last Breath

Silence hums a tender song,
As the night begins to throng.
Stars are dimming, one by one,
A soft embrace from the waking sun.

Shadows stretch and softly fade,
Wrapped in twilight's gentle shade.
The moon dips low, a silver sigh,
Whispering dreams as it says goodbye.

Echoes linger, soft and round,
In the quiet, peace is found.
Night's embrace, a fleeting kiss,
In fading hours, we find our bliss.

The dawn creeps in, a blush of light,
Welcoming day, bidding night goodnight.
With each breath, a new hope grows,
As the world awakens, life flows.

In the solitude, softly rest,
For in endings, we find our best.
The night yields to the day's bright call,
In this cycle, we rise, we fall.

Gleaming Tapestry of Colors

In a garden bright and fair,
Colors bloom beyond compare.
Petals dance in morning's breeze,
Nature's palette aims to please.

Crimson glows and sapphire sings,
Emerald drapes like vibrant wings.
Every hue a story tells,
In the quiet, beauty dwells.

Raindrops fall, they kiss the earth,
Giving life and joy, rebirth.
Sunshine kisses bud and leaf,
In the tapestry, beyond belief.

Season's change, but colors stay,
In hearts where memories lay.
Every blossom holds a dream,
In the garden, life's bright gleam.

So pause awhile, let colors inspire,
Feed your soul with love's sweet fire.
In this universe, vast and wide,
Find your peace, let colors guide.

The Birth of New Beginnings

In the silence of night's gentle sway,
Hope whispers softly, heralding day.
From ashes of dreams, new truths arise,
With grace and courage, we touch the skies.

The echoes of yesterday fade away,
Painting the future in hues of ray.
Seeds of tomorrow planted with care,
In gardens of faith, we're free to dare.

With each step forward, we break the mold,
Stories of heartbeats, yet to be told.
Embracing the light, we rise and stand,
Together united, hand in hand.

A fresh dawn beckons, a brand-new tune,
In the symphony played beneath the moon.
Let laughter and love be our guiding song,
As we weave our dreams where we belong.

With strength in the struggle, we learn to soar,
The past is a lesson, we're meant to explore.
Each moment a canvas, each breath a brush,
In the birth of beginnings, life's vibrant rush.

Day's First Breath

With the hush of night slowly fading,
The sun's embrace, a sweet invading.
Birds awaken, a jubilant choir,
Welcoming light as hopes inspire.

Veils of mist lift, secrets unfurl,
As dawn brings promise in golden swirl.
Soft whispers of wind in the trees,
Awakening dreams with gentle ease.

Light dances softly on the dew-kissed grass,
In this moment, all worries shall pass.
The canvas stretches, colors ignite,
Painting the heavens, pure and bright.

Children emerge with laughter and glee,
In the treasure of morning, they're wild and free.
Each face a story, each heart a song,
In the magic of morning, we all belong.

With every heartbeat, the day unfolds,
Each second a story, a treasure to hold.
In the hush of dawn, dreams take their flight,
In the day's first breath, we find our light.

Luminescence of Life

In shadows where light struggles to gleam,
The heart beats bright, igniting the dream.
Amidst the chaos, a glimmer appears,
In the luminescence, we wash away fears.

Stars above whisper tales of the night,
Echoes of moments, in shimmering light.
Each glimmer a story, each flicker a sigh,
In the dance of existence, learn how to fly.

Let the rhythm of life paint colors anew,
In laughter and tears, find strength to pursue.
With every embrace, a warm glowing spark,
In the luminescence, shine bright from the dark.

Through valleys of shadows, we travel with grace,
Finding the magic in every place.
Mirrors of friendship reflect our soul,
In the luminescence, we become whole.

Lift up your gaze, let your spirit ignite,
In the dance of the cosmos, be bold in the night.
Together we shine, together we thrive,
In the luminescence of being alive.

A Canvas of Dawn

With brushes dipped in shades of hope,
The sun rises high, teaching us to cope.
Each color a promise, each stroke a dream,
In the canvas of dawn, together we gleam.

Clouds drift like whispers across the sky,
As the world awakens, with a joyful sigh.
Nature sings softly, colors blend bright,
In the magic of morning, we take flight.

A palette of stories long left untold,
In every sunrise, our hearts unfold.
Embracing the gift of each brand-new day,
In the canvas of dawn, we find our way.

From the tender blush of peach to gold,
Each hue a memory that makes us bold.
With laughter as our brush, we paint and play,
In the canvas of dawn, let's celebrate today.

With open hearts, let the journey start,
In every moment, let love be our art.
As day's gentle whisper beckons us near,
On this canvas of dawn, we hold what is dear.

Dancing Lights of Dawn

Softly glows the morning ray,
Colors burst in bright display.
Birds awaken, sing their tune,
Chasing night away too soon.

Fields of gold and skies of blue,
Nature's canvas, fresh and new.
Whispers float on gentle breeze,
Dancing shadows 'neath the trees.

Every petal, dew-kissed bright,
Glistens in the morning light.
Joyful hearts rise with the sun,
A brand new day has begun.

Winds of change, they softly call,
Echoing in every hall.
Dancing lights in sweet ballet,
Guide our hopes along the way.

With each dawn, a promise blooms,
Chasing away the night's dark gloom.
In the light, together dwell,
Magic woven, all is well.

Whispers of the Morning Sky

Crimson blush upon the rise,
Whispers linger in the skies.
Clouds like dreams float soft and free,
Painting visions made to be.

Every star begins to fade,
In this serenade, displayed.
Gentle winds where silence sleeps,
Over valleys, softly creeps.

Golden rays touch every heart,
Poised to play their vital part.
Nature breathes a tender sigh,
Life awakens, fluttering high.

Splendid hues in morning's grace,
Fill each corner, every space.
With the dawn, a promise sworn,
In the joy of being born.

In this moment, still and bright,
Whispers guide the morning light.
Every glimmer shares the plea,
Let us cherish what will be.

Celestial Brushstrokes

Across the canvas, soft and wide,
Brushstrokes dance and gently glide.
Stars align, a twinkling thread,
Stories written, dreams unsaid.

Moonlit paths and sunsets steep,
Coloring the world in deep.
Where shadows play and silence gleams,
Awakening our hidden dreams.

Nature's palette, rich and bright,
Fills the heart with pure delight.
Every hue a tale to tell,
In this cosmic carousel.

Waves of color surging near,
In each stroke, the heart can hear.
A dance of light where spirits soar,
In this art, we seek for more.

Feel the magic brush the dawn,
In the light, our hopes are drawn.
Celestial beauty, ever near,
With every breath, we hold it dear.

Radiance Unveiled

From the shadows, whispers rise,
Dancing softly 'neath the skies.
Radiance unveils with each glance,
In the light, we find our chance.

Every color, bright and bold,
Tells a story yet untold.
In the stillness, magic flows,
Where the love of nature grows.

Heartbeats echo through the morn,
In this world, anew, reborn.
Every moment, pure and sweet,
Finding beauty in our feet.

Radiance twirls in perfect arcs,
Lighting paths, igniting sparks.
In the daylight, souls collide,
Together drawn by hope and pride.

With the dawn, all fears erase,
Leaving joy to take their place.
Radiance, with every breath,
Casts a light that conquers death.

Journey of the First Light

The dawn creeps softly on the land,
A whisper of warmth, a gentle hand.
Shadows flee as colors ignite,
In the quiet moments of first light.

Birds begin to sing their song,
Nature stirs, where dreams belong.
The world awakens from its night,
Bathed in the glow of hopeful light.

Waves of gold spill from the sun,
Tales of yesterdays now undone.
Each breath taken feels so right,
In the embrace of the new daylight.

Mountains stand with peaks so proud,
Wrapped in whispers of morning cloud.
Hearts beat strong, spirits take flight,
As we follow the journey of light.

With every step, a story told,
In hues of warmth, both bold and cold.
We dance beneath the sky's delight,
In the journey of the first light.

Brilliance Above the Trees

The sun dips low, the sky ignites,
With brilliant hues that take to flight.
Above the trees, the colors blend,
A masterpiece that knows no end.

Crimson, gold, and purple flow,
Painting the canvas of the glow.
Leaves shimmer with a soft embrace,
In the brilliance, they find their place.

Whispers of wind in gentle sway,
Guide the hearts that long to stay.
For in this moment, time stands still,
Above the trees, the world does thrill.

Stars twinkle as the shadows play,
In the darkness, hope finds its way.
Each sparkle tells a tale so free,
Of brilliance found above the trees.

As night ascends with velvet grace,
The moonlight dances in its place.
In dreams we roam, so wild and free,
Under the brilliance above the trees.

Kaleidoscope of Awakening

Morning breaks with sparkling hues,
A kaleidoscope of fresh views.
Each petal opens, a vibrant cheer,
Awakening life, drawing near.

Colors swirl in perfect design,
Nature's brush, a work divine.
A tapestry both bright and clear,
In this awakening, we draw near.

From dewdrops glistening on the grass,
To the sunbeams that brightly pass.
Every moment, a chance to see,
The magic in this tapestry.

With every heartbeat, colors shift,
Life evolves, a precious gift.
In this dance, we find our way,
In the kaleidoscope of today.

As day unfolds, we celebrate,
The beauty of the hand of fate.
Awake, alive, with spirits free,
In the kaleidoscope of memory.

Celestial Flare at Dawn

A flare ignites in morning's glow,
Celestial whispers start to flow.
Light spills forth, a gentle stream,
Waking the world, igniting dreams.

Birds take flight with wings outspread,
In harmony, where hopes are fed.
The sky ignites in shades of fire,
A chorus rising, sweet and dire.

Mountains echo with ancient calls,
As shadows dance along the walls.
Each ray a prayer, each beam a song,
In the dawn where we belong.

Colors burst, a radiant show,
Nature's canvas painted slow.
In every corner, life reborn,
In celestial flares as we adorn.

So rise with light, let spirits soar,
In the dawn's embrace, forevermore.
For in this moment, dreams align,
In the celestial flare, so divine.

Awakening to a New Palette

Morning breaks with colors bright,
Nature's canvas takes to flight.
Birds sing sweetly, life anew,
Brushstrokes blend in every hue.

Gentle winds begin to sway,
As shadows dance, they drift away.
The world awakes, a vibrant song,
And in this moment, we belong.

Soft pastels grace the sky,
Painting dreams as time slips by.
Each shade tells a tale entwined,
Of hope and joy, forever kind.

In whispers of the morning air,
Colors merge with tender care.
Awakening to life's embrace,
This palette blooms, a sacred space.

With every dawn, potential grows,
A masterpiece that softly glows.
In nature's art, we find our place,
Awakening to love's own grace.

The Sun's Gentle Rise

As the dawn whispers light,
The sun begins its gentle flight.
With golden rays, it paints the morn,
A new day's hope, reborn, adorned.

Clouds blush pink in soft embrace,
The world stirs in a quiet grace.
Each beam beckons, warm and wide,
Inviting dreams that now won't hide.

Day awakens from the night,
In the sun's tender light.
Shadows fall, and life ignites,
A dance of joy in soft delights.

The horizon glows with fiery hue,
Love and warmth, rebirth is true.
With every rise, a promise stays,
The sun will guide in myriad ways.

A gentle kiss upon the land,
The sun arises, bold and grand.
In its embrace, we find our way,
Together, we greet the new day.

Colors Embodied in Light

Light filters through the leafy trees,
Painting moments with every breeze.
Rich emeralds dance in delight,
As colors merge, kissed by the light.

Crisp blues stretch across the sky,
While golden rays on petals lie.
Nature's palette, vibrant, true,
Each day's art, forever new.

Crimson leaves in autumn's touch,
Brighten paths we cherish much.
With every shade, a story spins,
Of where the heart begins and wins.

In twilight's glow, soft whispers call,
As shadows blend and softly fall.
With every hue that fades away,
We hold the moments, come what may.

Colors wrapped in tender light,
Bathe the world in pure delight.
An everlasting dance we share,
In nature's heart, we find our care.

Whispering Flames of Dawn

Dawn breaks softly, flames arise,
Kissing the world with amber skies.
Flickers of hope begin to stir,
With each breath, the night's a blur.

Crimson embers light the way,
Through shadows, they begin to play.
Gentle whispers fill the air,
A promise lingers everywhere.

The horizon glows, a bold embrace,
Where warmth and wonder find their place.
In every flicker, stories weave,
Of moments lived and dreams conceived.

As daylight spills its golden grace,
The heart finds peace in this soft space.
Whispers of flames ignite the soul,
A dawn rebirth, our spirits whole.

With each new day, the fire speaks,
Of strength and love in subtle peaks.
Whispering flames of dawn ignite,
A canvas of dreams, pure delight.

Milton Keynes UK
Ingram Content Group UK Ltd.
UKHW010230111224
452348UK00011B/636